GW00383808

Moving House

BIBLE READINGS FOR SPECIAL TIMES

...for those times when we want to hear God's word speaking to us clearly

Catherine Hickey

Text copyright © Catherine Hickey 2006
The author asserts the moral right
to be identified as the author of this work

Published by
The Bible Reading Fellowship
First Floor, Elsfield Hall
15–17 Elsfield Way, Oxford OX2 8FG

ISBN-10 1 84101 457 5
ISBN-13 978 1 84101 457 9

First published 2006
10 9 8 7 6 5 4 3 2 1 0
All rights reserved

Acknowledgments
Unless otherwise indicated, scripture quotations are taken from the Holy
Bible, New International Version, copyright © 1973, 1978, 1984 by
International Bible Society, are used by permission of Hodder &
Stoughton Limited. All rights reserved. 'NIV' is a registered trademark of
International Bible Society. UK trademark number 1448790.

Scriptures quoted from the Good News Bible published by The Bible
Societies/HarperCollins Publishers Ltd, UK © American Bible Society
1966, 1971, 1976, 1992, used with permission.

Extract from 'The Lord is still in the city' by Carol Rowe ©, used by
permission.
Extract from meditation by Lois Siemens ©, used by permission.

A catalogue record for this book is available from the British Library

Printed by Gutenberg Press, Tarxien, Malta

Introduction

'Just at the moment the word "move" brings me out in a nervous rash.'

'I love moving. It is unusual for me to stay more than a year in one place.'

These are two very different reactions to moving house that I encountered recently. Perhaps moving is like Marmite: you either love it or hate it.

I don't think it is quite that simple. During the process of moving house, most of us experience a range of feelings. The circumstances of our move affect how we view it. The stage we are at in the process is a factor, too. The two people above were expressing how they felt at a particular moment—the first still unpacking and settling in, the second observing from a safe distance.

You may be just starting to think about moving, in the throes of the move or settling into a new home. Each stage brings its own stresses and joys. Today you may be loving it, tomorrow hating it—or vice versa.

Nowadays people move around much more than in the past. It is so commonplace that we may expect just to take it in our stride. But whether we move across continents or across town, it is a big upheaval. The whole process can take months or years. It is worth reflecting on what we are going through and inviting God to accompany us on the way.

Much of the Old Testament tells the story of people on the move. Abraham, Jacob and Joseph moved to new places as God formed the people of Israel. Under Moses' and Joshua's leadership, God brought the people out of Egypt, through the wilderness and into the land of Canaan. He later sent them into exile in Babylon. Through these moves God fulfilled his purposes for his people and, ultimately, for the whole world.

Movement is a feature of the New Testament, too, in the life of Jesus, his disciples and the early church. But in these notes I have concentrated on the Old Testament story as outlined above. There are many individual stories of significant moves that I have had to leave out. Ruth and Esther immediately come to mind. My focus on male characters is due to shortage of space rather than God's bias.

The Old Testament world was different from ours, but the people were as real as we are. They moved to real places, taking with them their families, belongings, hopes and fears. Like us, they were journeying through life, working out their relationship with God as they went. In their stories we find much that resonates with our own.

As I write this, I am living in Nepal with my family (Martin my husband, and our two children). We came here in 2002 to join the International Nepal Fellowship, a Christian health and development organization. Most of my life before that was spent in England. I moved once as a child, eight times as a single adult and four times after getting married. Some of these moves didn't take me far (from one rented house to another in the same part of town, for example), while others brought much greater change. But each involved endings and beginnings in some areas of my life.

Before coming to Nepal, we studied at All Nations Christian College in Hertfordshire. In preparation for moving overseas, we looked at the impact of change on our lives. Since then I have gone through a major move and seen others do the same. Looking back on my previous moves, I realize that, whatever distance we travel, in whatever season of life, there are many shared experiences.

In these 24 readings I reflect on different stages in the moving process. Rather than arranging them according to the chronology of a move, I have used the chronology of the Bible. This is to make the Bible the starting point and to draw out the exciting story it tells. The story is not yet finished—it will reach its culmination at the end of time. As moving house makes us focus on the here and now, I have included some passages that give this eternal perspective.

Moving house is never restful, but God says, 'My Presence will go with you, and I will give you rest' (Exodus 33:14). My prayer is that as you reflect on God's word you will enter into his presence and discover his rest.

Unless otherwise indicated, quotations are taken from the New International Version of the Bible.

GENESIS 12:1–3

Command and promise

The Lord had said to Abram, 'Leave your country, your people and your father's household and go to the land I will show you. I will make you into a great nation and I will bless you; I will make your name great, and you will be a blessing. I will bless those who bless you, and whoever curses you I will curse; and all peoples on earth will be blessed through you.'

God's command to Abram was twofold: he was commanded to *leave* all that was known to him—his country, people and family— and to *go* to a place that he didn't yet know. All moves, near or far, mean going from the familiar to the unfamiliar. Even moving back to a place where we have lived before, we will find ourselves stepping into the unknown. The place and people will have changed, or we will have changed, seeing things through different eyes.

In Abram's time and culture family roots were very important, and people had a strong sense of belonging. Leaving country, people and family was unusual. It required faith in the God who promised to show him the way. In our individualistic society, where mobility is the norm, our roots may not be so strong, but uprooting from a place where we feel we belong may be just as painful.

God's command to move was accompanied by a promise. God would make him into a great nation (Israel) and bless all peoples on earth through him (Jesus was an Israelite). Through Abram's obedience God would set in motion his plan to draw people from all nations to himself. As we move, we may feel led by God with a promise for the future, or we may feel pushed by circumstances and wonder if God is involved at all. Either way, we can trust God to fulfil his purposes for us and look for a promise for the times ahead.

'The Lord will fulfil his purpose for me; your love, O Lord, endures forever—do not abandon the works of your hands' (Psalm 138:8).

GENESIS 12:4–5

The effect on others

Abram was seventy-five years old when he set out from Haran. He took his wife Sarai, his nephew Lot, all the possessions they had accumulated and the people they had acquired in Haran and they set out for the land of Canaan.

Abram's move from Haran to Canaan sounds easy, but let's look closer. Abram took his wife and nephew with him. How did they feel about it? Were they called by God, too? What special friendships were they leaving behind? Lot and Sarai had already made one major move in their lives, from Ur to Haran (Genesis 11:31). Did this make it easier or harder to uproot a second time?

Abram left his father's household. His father, Terah, stayed in Haran and lived another 60 years. Did he oppose or support his son's move? Terah had taken the family to Haran, where they had prospered. Did he take Abram's departure as a rejection of all he'd done for him? Other Bible passages indicate that Terah worshipped other gods, so how did Abram explain his reason for leaving?

The Bible doesn't answer any of these questions, but it is clear that Abram's move affected the people going with him and those he left behind. How will our move affect the people in our lives? Even if we are not moving far, relationships will change, and we are sure to leave a gap in someone's life. Friends who outwardly support us may start to withdraw emotionally in the run-up to our move.

Abram was wealthy, with a large retinue of servants and staff (Genesis 14:14; 15:3). Moving all these people and belongings and travelling 450 miles south-west (from present-day Syria to Palestine) would have been a big operation. Moving is a big deal for us, too. It is not just about packing our possessions but dealing with the people in our lives. No wonder it is such a stressful event!

'Cast all your anxiety on him because he cares for you' (1 Peter 5:7).

GENESIS 12:11–13

Facing fears

As he was about to enter Egypt, he said to his wife Sarai, 'I know what a beautiful woman you are. When the Egyptians see you, they will say, "This is his wife." Then they will kill me but will let you live. Say you are my sister, so that I will be treated well for your sake and my life will be spared.'

Abram is remembered for his faith, but in this passage faith gives way to fear. Having passed briefly through Canaan Abram goes down to Egypt to escape a famine. Here he tells half-truths about his relationship with Sarai to protect himself. It is not an outright lie: Sarai is indeed his half-sister (Genesis 20:12). But Abram's dishonesty has serious consequences: Pharaoh takes Sarai as his wife and is severely punished by God (Genesis 12:14–20).

Why does Abram lose his trust in God and his integrity? Has he forgotten God's work in his life so far? Is he overwhelmed because he is somewhere new? Does he feel let down by God as things haven't worked out as he expected?

Our faith-filled lives can easily become fear-filled when we are moving to a new place. It is tough starting from scratch, and building new relationships in our neighbourhood, church or work takes time and effort. New responsibilities can stretch us to our limits. We may not fear death, but we may fear loneliness or failure. In our desire to be accepted, we may try to be something we're not.

When these insecurities surface, we need to turn to God—the one who truly knows us and has made us with our unique gifts, strengths and weaknesses. As we experience God's love and acceptance, we can be ourselves with others. Like Abram, we won't always get things right, but we will always have a God of grace nearby.

'For you created my inmost being; you knit me together in my mother's womb' (Psalm 139:13).

HEBREWS 11:8–10 (ABRIDGED)

A place to belong

By faith Abraham, when called to go to a place he would later receive as his inheritance, obeyed and went, even though he did not know where he was going. By faith he made his home in the promised land like a stranger in a foreign country; he lived in tents… For he was looking forward to the city with foundations, whose architect and builder is God.

After his stay in Egypt, Abraham (the new name given to Abram by God) moved back to Canaan, the promised land, where he lived for the best part of 100 years. He didn't settle in one of the city states, but lived in tents, moving his household and livestock from place to place. This was the only option for a newcomer, as the best land was already taken by farmers and city-dwellers.

I have lived in Nepal for over three years now as a 'stranger in a foreign country'. I'm not a tourist passing through—this is now my country of residence, and yet I don't really belong. My neighbours are friendly, but I am separated from them by culture, language, skin colour and other factors.

Moving can make us wonder where we belong. The place we used to live is no longer home, but we don't fit in the new place yet. Towards the end of his life, some of the people of Canaan called Abraham a 'mighty prince' (Genesis 23:6), but he still considered himself an 'alien and stranger' (23:4). He knew he was a temporary resident on this earth and his true home would be in heaven—a permanent city where God would dwell with his people (Revelation 21:2–4). Through Jesus, we too have this promise of an everlasting home. Let us remember this whenever we feel like a stranger in a foreign land: we can experience now our belonging in God.

'One thing I ask of the Lord, this is what I seek: that I may dwell in the house of the Lord all the days of my life' (Psalm 27:4).

GENESIS 27:41–43 (ABRIDGED)

Painful circumstances

Esau held a grudge against Jacob because of the blessing his father had given him. He said to himself, '… I will kill my brother Jacob.' When Rebekah was told what her older son Esau had said, she sent for her younger son Jacob and said to him, 'Your brother Esau is consoling himself with the thought of killing you… Flee at once to my brother Laban in Haran.'

Jacob, Abraham's grandson, moved from Canaan back to Haran, but not out of choice. His relationship with his twin brother Esau was broken, and his life was threatened. But Jacob wasn't an innocent victim: his own deceit in tricking Esau out of their father's blessing (Genesis 27:1–40) was the reason for Esau's anger.

Sometimes we move for negative reasons, in circumstances beyond our control, or of our own making, or a combination of both. We face the future with grief and dread. We may regret our own mistakes, feel anger at others or be disappointed with God.

For Jacob, though, this isn't the end of the story. On the journey to Haran he hears God's voice. In Haran he finds love and begins a family of his own. He is cheated by Laban, but through hard work and God's blessing he prospers. He grows through his struggles, developing a humble, grateful heart and a strength of spirit. After 20 years he returns to Canaan and is reconciled with Esau. But then his wife Rachel dies and he loses his favourite son, Joseph. After enduring famine in Canaan he is reunited with Joseph in Egypt. On his death bed he prays to 'the God who has been my shepherd all my life to this day' (Genesis 48:15).

Whatever our pain or our mistakes, may we not cease to journey with God. May we encounter him in the twists and turns of life, growing into the person he wants us to be.

'The Lord is my shepherd, I shall not be in want' (Psalm 23:1).

GENESIS 28:13–15 (ABRIDGED)

God's big picture

'I am the Lord, the God of your father Abraham and the God of Isaac. I will give you and your descendants the land on which you are lying. Your descendants will be like the dust of the earth… All peoples on earth will be blessed through you and your offspring. I am with you and will watch over you wherever you go.'

On his way to Haran, Jacob stops for the night, and dreams of a stairway reaching from earth to heaven. In his dream, God speaks the promise above. First, God reminds Jacob that he is the God of Abraham and Isaac. He then gives Jacob the same promise he gave to his grandfather and father (Genesis 17:8; 26:2–5). He will give Jacob's descendants the land of Canaan and through them he will bless all peoples on earth. Through Jesus, a descendant of Jacob, God's blessing would eventually extend to all nations.

It may have seemed as if Jacob had lost the plot, but God hadn't. Through this young man who had tricked his father and cheated his brother, God would fulfil his ultimate plan—to bless the nations. God always has the big picture; we only see a small part. If the move we are making isn't part of our game plan, let's remember that it might be part of God's. For God, no situation is hopeless or beyond his redemption.

In Jacob's time, different gods were associated with different people and places. Jacob's relatives in Haran worshipped other gods, and he may have feared that in leaving Canaan he was leaving behind the God of Abraham and Isaac. But God will be with Jacob wherever he goes—he is the God of the whole world. Wherever we are or whatever we face, God is with us.

'Where can I flee from your presence? … If I settle on the far side of the sea, even there your hand will guide me' (Psalm 139:7, 9–10).

GENESIS 28:16–19 (ABRIDGED)

The Lord is in this place

When Jacob awoke from his sleep, he thought, 'Surely the Lord is in this place, and I was not aware of it.' He was afraid and said, 'How awesome is this place! This is none other than the house of God…' Early the next morning Jacob took the stone he had placed under his head and set it up as a pillar and poured oil on top of it. He called that place Bethel.

When Jacob stopped for the night, it was dark, so he probably didn't take in his surroundings. When he awakes, that same nondescript place is 'awesome' in his eyes. What has made the difference? He has realized that God is there. Realizing that God is with us can change our perspective on the place in which we live.

God reveals himself in lots of ways. One is through his creation. I love gazing at the Himalayas: they remind me of God's majesty. I love looking out to sea: it reminds me of God's vastness and power. But I have lived most of my life in urban areas, without such beautiful reminders of God's presence. As a student I attended a church on a high-rise city housing estate. The believers there sang a song with the chorus: 'The Lord is still in the city, in the pain, in the rush, in the noise. The Lord is still in the city—listen, you will hear his voice.' They saw God at work and heard his voice in that grey corner of their city. When we encounter God in his word and his work, we too can say, 'Surely the Lord is in this place.'

Jacob set up a stone pillar as a memorial in the place where he heard God's voice, and consecrated it with oil. Bethel means House of God and it remained a special place for Jacob (Genesis 31:13). Keeping a record of our encounters with God reminds us of his presence and can make even the most average place 'awesome'.

'You will seek me and find me when you seek me with all your heart' *(Jeremiah 29:13).*

GENESIS 31:26–28 (ABRIDGED)

Facing goodbyes

Then Laban said to Jacob, '… Why did you run off secretly and deceive me? Why didn't you tell me, so that I could send you away with joy and singing to the music of tambourines and harps? You didn't even let me kiss my grandchildren and my daughters goodbye. You have done a foolish thing.'

After 20 years in Haran, God tells Jacob to return to Canaan. He has married two of Laban's daughters and accumulated livestock in spite of his uncle's efforts to cheat him. Fearing further trickery on Laban's part, Jacob steals away without saying goodbye.

No one likes goodbyes. Jacob had good reason to avoid them, and we may wish to as well. We may fear lifting the lid on our emotions, especially if we are already stressed by the move. If we are leaving a difficult situation, it can seem easier to slip off unnoticed.

Jacob's quick departure was understandable, but it was a kind of deception. If we want to do the same, we need to ask, 'Who am I trying to kid?' The pain of leaving will hit us eventually; unresolved issues will catch up with us, just as Laban caught up with Jacob.

Goodbyes are important, for those leaving and those staying behind. They recognize special relationships and bring closure. In Nepal, those leaving are honoured with garlands and invitations to eat *dal bhat*, the national dish. The ritual of the office whipround and presentation serves the same purpose. Before leaving England we held a 'goodbye party'. We also walked around the town, saying goodbye to places—school, supermarket, park, church, chip shop.

When Laban found Jacob, all was not resolved, but they made an agreement before God and ate together. Then, Laban blessed his grandchildren and daughters and went home (Genesis 31:51–55).

'Let love and faithfulness never leave you…then you will win favour and a good name in the sight of God and man' (Proverbs 3:3–4).

GENESIS 37:23–28 (ABRIDGED)

Identity crisis

So when Joseph came to his brothers, they stripped him of his robe—the richly ornamented robe he was wearing—and they took him and threw him into the cistern… As they sat down to eat their meal, they looked up and saw a caravan of Ishmaelites coming from Gilead… [his brothers] pulled Joseph up out of the cistern and sold him… to the Ishmaelites.

Joseph was a secure young man. He was Jacob's favourite son and had a multi-coloured coat to prove it. Then he was stripped of his robe and his place in the family and sold as a slave.

When we move, we can feel stripped of the things that give us security and status. Before, we felt included in our circle of friends, church or workplace. Now we have relinquished these roles and the recognition they brought. As a result, we may wonder who we are.

I lived for ten years in north London, first as a single person, then married, then as a mother. I had colleagues and friends who knew me as an individual. Then we moved as a family to start at Bible college. Suddenly we were known as 'the Hickeys'. No one asked me anything about myself. It started to bug me. I wanted to be known for who I was—I wanted recognition.

Men and women, single or married, and children too, can experience an identity crisis when they move. David Pollock says that feeling 'statusless, structureless and clueless' are features of transition. Anxiety, grief and loss of self-esteem are common, too. We can imagine Joseph feeling all these things as he set off with the Ishmaelites. Whatever our age and experience, we become learners again. We have to get to know the area, the social networks, the office culture. Meanwhile, like Joseph, we are in a vulnerable place.

'The Lord is my strength and my shield; my heart trusts in him, and I am helped' (Psalm 28:7).

GENESIS 41:39–41 (ABRIDGED)

Re-evaluating roles

**Pharaoh said to Joseph, 'Since God has made all this known
to you, there is no-one so discerning and wise as you…
I hereby put you in charge of the whole land of Egypt.'**

Joseph was 17 years old when he was taken to Egypt as a slave. At
the age of 30, he was put in charge of the whole land. How did this
happen? Joseph had God-given gifts of wisdom and discernment,
seen in his ability to interpret dreams and also in his management
skills. As he used these gifts, God blessed the things he did.

First Joseph was sold to Potiphar, an Egyptian official. Potiphar
saw that 'the Lord was with him' and eventually put him in charge
of all his affairs. Joseph was wrongly imprisoned but the warder
saw that 'the Lord was with him' and put him in charge of prison
affairs. When Joseph interpreted Pharaoh's dreams, Pharaoh too
recognized his special gifts. It took 13 years and some difficult
experiences before Joseph was able to fulfil his God-given potential.

It can take us time to discover our gifts and use them as God
intended. We may have a job or responsibilities that don't fit our
abilities or interests—through lack of choice, pressure from ourselves or others, not knowing where our gifts lie or not accepting
how God has made us. Moving gives us a chance to re-evaluate
our lives and ask, 'What are my gifts? How can I best use them?'

Let us reflect on our abilities, interests, heart's desires and
passions. After moving, we may want to create a new role for
ourselves quickly, but there is value in taking our time if possible.
Even if opportunities seem limited, we should resolve to discover
and use our gifts wherever we can. After all, Joseph was a slave and
a prisoner before he was put in charge of the land.

'Whoever can be trusted with very little can also be trusted with much'
(Luke 16:10).

EXODUS 3:9–10

Called to a task

'And now the cry of the Israelites has reached me, and I have seen the way the Egyptians are oppressing them. So now, go. I am sending you to Pharaoh to bring my people the Israelites out of Egypt.'

It is a few hundred years since Joseph's family followed him to Egypt. There, the Israelites increased in numbers until a new Pharaoh made them slaves. Moses had grown up in Egypt but had fled. Now God calls him to return on a special mission.

Does God have a special mission for you? Some move with a strong sense of calling to a particular task. Others become aware of God's purpose for them after they arrive. But many people don't realize that God has work for them to do. All Jesus' followers are called to play a part in making disciples. Our mission may be to bring the light of Jesus into our workplace, to show God's love to a neighbour, to challenge an injustice, or to build up other believers. We are called not because we are special but because we serve a special God who has chosen to involve us in his work.

Moses didn't feel up to the task and he raised lots of objections. Who am I to do this? What shall I say to the people? What if they don't believe me or listen to me? I've never been a good speaker! God assures Moses that he will be with him but still Moses pleads, 'O Lord, please send someone else to do it' (Exodus 3:11—4:13).

Eventually Moses set off for Egypt with his wife and sons. Through his obedience, God fulfilled his plan for the Israelites. The exodus from Egypt forged their identity as God's people. The Israelites had been crying to God for deliverance so he sent Moses. Your arrival may also be the answer to someone's heartfelt prayers.

'You did not choose me, but I chose you and appointed you to go and bear fruit—fruit that will last' (John 15:16).

DEUTERONOMY 1:6–8 (ABRIDGED)

God's timing

The Lord our God said to us at Horeb, 'You have stayed long enough at this mountain. Break camp and advance into the hill country of the Amorites… Go in and take possession of the land that the Lord swore he would give to your fathers.'

The Israelites arrived at Mount Sinai (Horeb) three months after leaving Egypt. The following year, God told them to move on, and he scheduled their journey: 'Whenever the cloud lifted from above the Tent, the Israelites set out; wherever the cloud settled, the Israelites encamped.' However long the cloud settled, they encamped and set out 'at the Lord's command' (Numbers 9:17, 23).

We need to seek and trust God's timing. Maybe a change in circumstances is the catalyst for our move. We may move for our children's schooling or downsize upon retirement. Having moved, we may intend to stay put for a while! God has given us choice and common sense, but we should submit our plans to him—and be prepared for his plans and timing to be different from ours.

Recently, some colleagues explained how God has shown them it is time to leave Nepal. He has spoken through circumstances, the Bible and trusted friends. He has given both husband and wife an inner conviction about the move. Their lives in Nepal are fulfilled but they have heeded the warning they heard in prayer: 'If you overstay your time in Nepal, the Lord's anointing will leave you.'

The Israelites' stay at Mount Sinai had been a special time. God had given them laws to govern their lives. He had expressed his commitment to them and shown that he expected them to worship him alone. Yet, he didn't want them to stay there for ever. Whether we have been at a particular 'mountain' for some time or have just arrived, let us 'break camp and advance' when God speaks.

'There is… a season for every activity under heaven' (Ecclesiastes 3:1).

———————————— MONDAY ————————————

NUMBERS 1:1–4 (ABRIDGED)

Practical preparations

The Lord spoke to Moses… on the first day of the second month of the second year after the Israelites came out of Egypt. He said; 'Take a census of the whole Israelite community by their clans and families, listing every man by name… One man from each tribe… is to help you.'

Lists seem to be a feature of every move, whether you keep them in your head, on the back of an envelope or on a palm-top computer.

God is practical. He gave Moses these instructions 20 days before the Israelites left Sinai. The purpose of the census was to show the numbers of fighting men. God also gave instructions for the arrangement of the tents, duties within the camp and purifying the camp. He told Moses to celebrate Passover before leaving, and to make trumpets to call the people together and signal departure. Having prepared well, the Israelites could set off in an orderly way.

It is interesting to see how different people go about moving. Some begin their practical preparations six months in advance while others leave it to the last minute. Either approach is fine, but when things are so chaotic that lots of unfinished business is left for others, it can cause resentment and mar happy memories.

God tells Moses to enlist some help to get the work done on time. Most of us tend to ask for too little help. If you have children, sharing out some tasks is a good way for them to feel involved. But moving with a family can mean allowing for different organizational styles. My husband likes to finish one job before starting the next. There is method in my multi-tasking madness, but he doesn't see it. If organization is not your strength, ask God for help—the God who, at the beginning of time, created order from chaos.

'My grace is sufficient for you, for my power is made perfect in weakness' (2 Corinthians 12:9).

NUMBERS 13:17–20 (ABRIDGED)

Thinking ahead

*When Moses sent them to explore Canaan, he said: '… See
what the land is like and whether the people who live there are
strong or weak, few or many. What kind of land do they live
in? Is it good or bad? What kind of towns do they live in? Are
they walled or fortified? How is the soil? Is it fertile or poor?'*

When the Israelites arrived at the edge of the promised land,
Moses sent twelve spies to find out what lay ahead.

'Exploring the land' is an important part of moving. Most
people check out all aspects of the neighbourhood before deciding
where to live. Even if the decision isn't ours, we'll probably want
to know something about where we're going. This is important for
emotional as well as practical reasons. Emotionally, a move can
take many months. Our possessions may make the journey in a
day but our hearts and minds need longer to leave one place and
settle in another. Those who move at very short notice often have
some emotional catching up to do later.

As our move approaches, we need to start disengaging from our
current life and looking ahead. Keeping present and future in
balance can be difficult. Some of us will not give much thought to
the future. Getting everything packed up and in the removal van is
the end we have in sight! We forget that this end is also a beginning.
Others may over-emphasize the future, avoiding the pain of leaving
or building up unrealistic expectations about what lies ahead.

Moses gave the spies a list of questions. What questions do we
need to ask now in preparation? Someone I know compiles a photo
album before returning home from Nepal. She contacts friends and
the children's school and builds up a picture, literally, of what lies
ahead. Knowing what to expect helps the whole family to adjust.

'The plans of the diligent lead to profit' (Proverbs 21:5).

Facing discouragement

They gave Moses this account: 'We went into the land to which you sent us, and it does flow with milk and honey! Here is its fruit. But the people who live there are powerful, and the cities are fortified and very large.'

After 40 days the spies returned from Canaan. They arrived carrying grapes, pomegranates and figs, which they showed the people as they gave the above report. They had found a good land, just as God had promised. But then their focus switched from the fruit of the land to the fortified cities and warrior people they had seen.

The Israelites may have expected moving into Canaan to be easy. After all, God had promised them the land. The twelve spies see opposition ahead and are hugely discouraged, concluding, 'We can't attack these people as they are stronger than we are'.

As we move, we may find things are not as we expected. Maybe our new job isn't quite what we were led to believe. Maybe our house has problems the survey didn't reveal. Perhaps our church isn't as friendly as we had hoped or our neighbours play their music too loud. Like the Israelites, we may fear the 'battles' ahead.

Perhaps we expect too much of ourselves. People moving into overseas mission sometimes hope to 'hit the ground running'. Instead they hit the challenges of living in a new culture and climate. Moving takes its toll in any part of the world, and we should set ourselves manageable goals.

The spies forgot God's promise to be with us in our battles. They exaggerated the negative, losing all perspective: 'The land we explored *devours* those living in it. *All* the people… are of great size… We seemed like *grasshoppers*…' (Numbers 13:32–33, my italics). Let's focus on the positive instead and keep a right perspective.

'Those who hope in the Lord will renew their strength' (Isaiah 40:31).

NUMBERS 14:1–3

Turning to God

That night all the people of the community raised their voices and wept aloud. All the Israelites grumbled against Moses and Aaron, and the whole assembly said to them, 'If only we had died in Egypt! Or in this desert! Why is the Lord bringing us to this land only to let us fall by the sword?'

Hearing the spies' report, the Israelites hit rock bottom. 'Where can we go? Our brothers have made us lose heart,' they complained (Deuteronomy 1:28). We often go through a 'honeymoon' period when we move. Everything is different, exciting, full of potential. Then suddenly the place that promised so much is full of problems. In any transition we will hit a low, sooner or later. We may feel like victims, seeing no way forward. We may become critical of our new place, others or God. This doesn't mean our move was a mistake.

A key to moving forward is to adjust our expectations to the reality we face, accepting our new life and committing ourselves to it. This may happen naturally over time or it may take conscious effort. Developing supportive friendships can make a big difference.

When we are feeling low, it is OK to ask questions of God. He encourages us to pour out our hearts to him. Sadly, the Israelites turned their hearts away from God. They questioned his character and his love for them: 'The Lord hates us; so he brought us out of Egypt to deliver us into the hands of the Amorites to destroy us.'

God was angry, but he didn't destroy the Israelites. Instead, he delayed their entry into Canaan by 40 years, until the people of that generation had died—'in the desert' as they had wished!

Let us bring our struggles to the God who loves us and keeps his promises to us. Let us not turn away from him or delay the blessings he has in store for us.

'Pour out your hearts to him, for God is our refuge' (Psalm 62:8b).

JOSHUA 1:1–3 (ABRIDGED)

Exciting challenges

*After the death of Moses the servant of the Lord, the Lord said
to Joshua… 'Moses my servant is dead. Now then, you and all
these people, get ready to cross the Jordan River into the land
I am about to give to them—to the Israelites. I will give you
every place where you set your foot, as I promised Moses.'*

We have looked at the problems we may face when moving, but
let's not forget the excitement and opportunities of a new start!

After 40 years wandering in the desert, the Israelites arrived at
the river Jordan, opposite Canaan. Joshua was one of the twelve
original spies, but he opposed the people's rebellion and so lived
to enter the promised land (Numbers 14:6–9, 30, 38).

Finally, God's promise to Abraham was to be fulfilled! Joshua
sounds excited as he orders, 'Get your supplies ready. Three days
from now you will… take possession of the land' (Joshua 1:11).

God was calling Joshua to personal growth. Moses had led the
people across the Red Sea. Joshua would lead them across the
river Jordan. He probably didn't need reminding that Moses was
dead, but God made the point anyway! Joshua was now in
charge—it was time for him to be stretched as never before.

Crossing the flooded Jordan was just the first of the challenges
he faced as leader of the Israelites. Many more awaited him as he
led them in battle in Canaan. Joshua must have been nervous
because three times in this chapter God commands, 'Be strong
and courageous', promising to be with him wherever he goes.

God calls us to growth as we face new situations. Like Joshua,
we may have to develop new skills and confidence. 'Our faith is
designed to grow until the day we die,' a colleague reminds me. Let
us be strong and courageous, seizing all opportunities for growth.

'If God is for us, who can be against us?' (Romans 8:31).

JOSHUA 24:14–15 (ABRIDGED)

Choose whom you will serve

Fear the Lord and serve him with all faithfulness. Throw away the gods your forefathers worshipped beyond the River and in Egypt, and serve the Lord… Choose for yourselves… whom you will serve, whether the gods your forefathers served beyond the River, or the gods of the Amorites, in whose land you are living. As for me and my household, we will serve the Lord.

God loved the Israelites and wanted their wholehearted devotion in return. This was the covenant he made when he gave his law to Moses on Mount Sinai. Both Moses and Joshua gathered the people together at key times so they could remember this covenant of love and rededicate themselves to God. On one such occasion, Joshua issued this challenge to serve the Lord 'with all faithfulness'.

The Israelites' forefathers, who came from the other side of the River Euphrates, worshipped a moon god. The Egyptians worshipped a sun god. The local people (Amorites) worshipped weather and fertility gods. But the Israelites were called to worship the Lord who ruled the moon and sun, the weather and the fertility of animals and land. Although these 'gods' were false, they posed a real threat to the people's relationship with God. The Israelites were settling down to farm the land, so the Canaanite gods seemed like useful friends. The Lord had been faithful to them in the wilderness and in battle, but was he sufficient for their new agricultural life?

Has our faith in God been wrapped up in a particular place or past experience? As we move, are we being enticed by new 'gods'— anything that takes the Lord's rightful place in our hearts and lives? Are there 'gods' we have worshipped in the past that we can now 'throw away' as we start somewhere new? Like Joshua and the Israelites, we are free to choose who, or what, we will serve.

'Yield your hearts to the Lord, the God of Israel' (Joshua 24:23).

PSALM 137:1–4 (ABRIDGED)

Grieving for the past

By the rivers of Babylon we sat and wept when we remembered Zion. There on the poplars we hung our harps, for there… our tormentors demanded songs of joy; they said, 'Sing us one of the songs of Zion!' How can we sing the songs of the Lord while in a foreign land?

Once settled in Canaan, the Israelites built a temple in Jerusalem, or Zion, where they worshipped the Lord. But they also followed the religious practices of the Canaanites. Moral decline led to social and political decline and they came under increasing pressure from the nations around them. At last, the Babylonians invaded, destroying Jerusalem and its temple, and carrying the people into exile.

In Babylon the Israelites were overcome by grief when they thought of Jerusalem. We too may grieve for what we have lost, even if we feel positive about our move, as Lois Siemens describes:

The grief I was experiencing… seemed abnormal but it wasn't… This was not just about changing address or missing people. This was about changing answers to long held questions of where I'm from… what I believe, who I am. It encompassed issues of identity, place and home.

The Israelites' identity as God's chosen people had been bound up with his promised land. Who were they now in this foreign land?

Places are important to us. We are moulded by them; we leave our mark on them; they hold memories. Whenever my husband Martin returns to Bradford, he drives past the house where he spent his childhood. The lilac bush his parents planted when he was born still stands in the front garden. It still feels like his home.

Eventually the Israelites were able to worship the Lord in Babylon. Their worship became more important than their whereabouts.

'God is king over all the world; praise him…!' (Psalm 47:7, GNB).

JEREMIAH 29:5–7 (ABRIDGED)

Settling in

Build houses and settle down; plant gardens and eat what they produce. Marry and have sons and daughters… Increase in number there; do not decrease. Also, seek the peace and prosperity of the city to which I have carried you… Pray to the Lord for it, because if it prospers, you too will prosper.

We say that 'home is where the heart is'. The Israelites were in Babylon, but their heart was in Zion and they longed to return. The prophet Jeremiah wrote to tell them they would be in exile for 70 years. They needed to settle down in Babylon.

After moving, how do we settle down and feel at home? Jeremiah gives very practical advice. We may not need to build our house, but we can try to make our new place as we'd like it. A bit of gardening can help us feel rooted. Even if marriage is not on the horizon, we can build relationships and look for growth in our lives.

When all else is new, familiar pastimes, routines or traditions help us settle. One family who moved a lot always unpacked their waffle maker and sat down to a special breakfast on their first day in a new house. You may prefer an early morning run, walking the dog, or a lie-in reading the papers!

If we only expect to stay a short while, we may be reluctant to invest too much in our new neighbourhood. But it is important that we get involved—seeking the 'peace and prosperity' of the community where we live now. As we pray for a place, our heart moves in. At times we may wish we were somewhere else. We may think that 'the grass is greener on the other side of the fence'. But in fact the grass is greener where we water it.

'He turned the desert into pools of water and the parched ground into flowing springs; there he brought the hungry to live, and they founded a city where they could settle' (Psalm 107:35–36).

ISAIAH 52:9–10

Making things new

*Burst into songs of joy together, you ruins of Jerusalem, for
the Lord has comforted his people, he has redeemed
Jerusalem. The Lord will lay bare his holy arm in the sight of
all the nations, and all the ends of the earth will see the
salvation of our God.*

When the Persian king Cyrus came to power in Babylon, he sent
the Israelites back to their homeland, where they rebuilt the
temple in Jerusalem and the city walls. The people experienced
great joy when they rediscovered God's law but before long they
were compromising their faith again (Nehemiah 8:12; 13:6–31).

As we move, we may have hopes for a new start or a bright
new future, as the returning Israelites probably did. Our move may
bring us many good things: a new home, new friendships, new
opportunities. But some of the old will come too: old patterns of
behaviour, longstanding fears and failings, difficult relationships
perhaps. I am reminded of a song by the pop group Crowded
House: 'Everywhere you go, you always take the weather with you'.

In the passage above, Isaiah looks beyond the physical
rebuilding of Jerusalem to a greater restoration and redemption.
Jesus, through his death on the cross, has extended salvation to
all the nations. Jerusalem was the Israelites' city, but the 'new
Jerusalem' (Revelation 21:2) will be a place of joy for *all* people.

God says, 'I will create new heavens and a new earth… I will
create Jerusalem to be a delight and its people a joy… the sound of
weeping… will be heard in it no more' (Isaiah 65:17–19). This is
the future that awaits us. In the meantime Jesus will begin his work
of restoration and rebuilding in our lives now, as we invite him.

*'He who was seated on the throne said, "I am making everything new"'
(Revelation 21:5).*

EPHESIANS 2:19–22 (ABRIDGED)

God's dwelling place

You are no longer foreigners and aliens, but fellow-citizens with God's people and members of God's household... with Christ Jesus himself as the chief cornerstone. In him the whole building is joined together and rises to become a holy temple in the Lord. And in him you too are being built together to become a dwelling in which God lives by his Spirit.

In his letter to the Ephesians, Paul explains that, through Christ, both Jews and non-Jews have been brought close to God. Faith in Jesus is now the criterion for being one of God's people, and those who were 'foreigners' are now 'fellow-citizens'. As Christians we are members of God's household, wherever our move may take us.

The Israelites worshipped God in a temple. Now God's people are that temple—the place where God dwells (see Revelation 21:3). As God's people on earth we can have a foretaste of God living among us. God's purpose for us is that 'through the church, the manifold wisdom of God should be made known to the rulers and authorities in the heavenly realms' (Ephesians 3:10).

Do we have such a high view of the church? Some reduce it to a social club where they can meet like-minded people. Some have had unhappy experiences in churches which have left them disillusioned. Some say, 'I'm a Christian but I don't go to church.'

There are many different ways of being church. As we move, we can look for somewhere that suits us. But sometimes there won't be much choice, and we may have to settle for something that seems less than ideal. Or the 'perfect' church we join may turn out to be less than perfect after all! Let us engage with God's people wherever we are and expect to be built into a 'dwelling in which God lives by his Spirit'.

'Let us not give up meeting together' (Hebrews 10:25).

DEUTERONOMY 8:11–14 (ABRIDGED)

Remember God's goodness

*Be careful that you do not forget the Lord your God,
failing to observe his commands… that I am giving you
this day. Otherwise, when you eat and are satisfied,
when you build fine houses and settle down, and when your
herds and flocks grow large and your silver and gold
increase… then your heart will become proud
and you will forget the Lord your God.*

How quick we are to forget what God has done for us! Before the Israelites entered Canaan, Moses gave them this warning. They had spent 40 years wandering in the wilderness, depending on God to guide them and provide for them. But Moses knew they risked forgetting the Lord once they became more self-sufficient.

Moving house has probably made us rely on God in new ways, as we have faced uncertainty, change and other challenges. But if our move has brought greater material comfort, it can make us proud and independent, as Moses went on to say: 'You may say to yourself, "My power and the strength of my hands have produced this wealth for me". But remember the Lord your God, for it is he who gives you the ability to produce wealth' (8:17–18).

Remembering what God has done is a recurrent theme in the Old Testament. Many of the Psalms retell the story of God rescuing the people from Egypt and bringing them into the promised land (Psalms 78, 105, 114 and 136, for example). Our movements may not seem as dramatic as those of the Israelites, but we too need to remember how God has guided and helped us.

When the Israelites remembered God's goodness, they were more inclined to keep his commands. For us too, remembering God's loving care helps us to walk in loving obedience to him.

'Praise the Lord, O my soul, and forget not all his benefits' (Psalm 103:2).

JOHN 14:2–3

Looking to the future

'In my Father's house are many rooms; if it were not so,
I would have told you. I am going there to prepare a place for
you. And if I go and prepare a place for you, I will come back
and take you to be with me that you also may be where I am.'

In 1984 the British director Jack Gold made a film called *The Chain*, about seven interconnected house moves taking place on the same day in London. At the start of the film a lodger moves out of his rented room in an East End house into the house he is buying with his girlfriend. The comedy shows different people moving higher up the property ladder. Finally a wealthy old man leaves his large house to move back into the same room the lodger occupied—in the East End house where he grew up. His life has gone full circle.

In Eastern thought, life is circular, as people are reborn again and again in different forms. These ideas have taken hold in the West, too: the theme song for Disney's *Lion King* is 'The circle of life'. But the Bible tells us that we are not going round and round in circles: we are heading somewhere.

We have looked at the new Jerusalem, but here Jesus uses the imagery of a house, not a city. God is building a people, but each individual is important. Jesus is preparing a room for us in his Father's house. How do we get there? Jesus replies, 'I am the way… No-one comes to the Father except through me' (John 14:6).

Today you may be feeling energized or exhausted by your move. God promised Moses, 'My Presence will go with you, and I will give you rest' (Exodus 33:14). Let us discover God's presence and enter his rest each day of our lives. And let us follow Jesus to that place where we can live in God's presence and his rest for eternity.

'Surely goodness and love will follow me all the days of my life, and I will dwell in the house of the Lord for ever' (Psalm 23:6).

Bible reading notes from BRF

If you have found this booklet helpful and would like to continue reading the Bible regularly, you may like to explore BRF's three series of Bible reading notes.

NEW DAYLIGHT

New Daylight offers a devotional approach to reading the Bible. Each issue covers four months of daily Bible readings and reflection from a regular team of contributors, who represent a stimulating mix of church backgrounds. Each day's reading provides a Bible passage (text included), comment and prayer or thought for reflection. In *New Daylight* the Sundays and special festivals from the church calendar are noted on the relevant days, to help you appreciate the riches of the Christian year.

DAY BY DAY WITH GOD

Day by Day with God (published jointly with Christina Press) is written especially for women, with a regular team of contributors. Each four-monthly issue offers daily Bible readings, with key verses printed out, helpful comment, a prayer or reflection for the day ahead, and suggestions for further reading.

GUIDELINES

Guidelines is a unique Bible reading resource that offers four months of in-depth study written by leading scholars. Contributors are drawn from around the world, as well as the UK, and they represent a thought-provoking breadth of Christian tradition. *Guidelines* is written in weekly units consisting of six sections plus an introduction and a final section of points for thought and prayer.

If you would like to subscribe to one or more of these sets of Bible reading notes, please use the order form overleaf.

NOTES SUBSCRIPTIONS

❏ I would like to give a gift subscription (please complete both name and address sections below)

❏ I would like to take out a subscription myself (complete name and address details only once)

This completed coupon should be sent with appropriate payment to BRF. Alternatively, please write to us quoting your name, address, the subscription you would like for either yourself or a friend (with their name and address), the start date and credit card number, expiry date and signature if paying by credit card.

Gift subscription name _____

Gift subscription address_____

_____Postcode _____

Please send beginning with the January / May / September issue: (delete as applicable)

(please tick box)	UK	SURFACE	AIR MAIL
NEW DAYLIGHT	❏ £12.00	❏ £13.35	❏ £15.60
GUIDELINES	❏ £12.00	❏ £13.35	❏ £15.60
DAY BY DAY WITH GOD	❏ £12.75	❏ £14.10	❏ £16.35

Please complete the payment details below and send your coupon, with appropriate payment to: **BRF, First Floor, Elsfield Hall, 15–17 Elsfield Way, Oxford OX2 8FG.**

Your name _____

Your address_____

_____Postcode _____

Total enclosed £ _____ (cheques made payable to 'BRF')

Payment: cheque ❏ postal order ❏ Visa ❏ Mastercard ❏ Switch ❏

Card number: ☐☐☐☐☐☐☐☐☐☐☐☐☐☐☐☐

Expiry date of card: ☐☐☐☐   Issue number (Switch): ☐☐☐☐

Signature (essential if paying by credit/Switch card)

❏ Please do not send me further information about BRF publications.

BRF resources are available from your local Christian bookshop. BRF is a Registered Charity

Sometimes you need more than a card…

BIBLE READINGS FOR SPECIAL TIMES

Bereavement

Jean Watson

BIBLE READINGS FOR SPECIAL TIMES

Ill Health

Wendy Bray

BIBLE READINGS FOR SPECIAL TIMES

Marriage

Anna and Nick Brooker

BIBLE READINGS FOR SPECIAL TIMES

Retirement

David Winter

Confirmation

BIBLE READINGS FOR SPECIAL TIMES

Mike Starkey

Going to College

BIBLE READINGS FOR SPECIAL TIMES

Michael Volland

Moving House

BIBLE READINGS FOR SPECIAL TIMES

Catherine Hickey

New Baby

BIBLE READINGS FOR SPECIAL TIMES

Lindsay Melluish

Bible Readings for Special Times are available from your local Christian bookshop or from BRF using the order form on page 32

visit www.brf.org.uk

Christian bookshops: All Christian bookshops stock BRF publications.
Telephone: To place your order, dial 01865 319700.
Fax: To place your order, dial 01865 319701.
Web: To place your order using the BRF website, visit www.brf.org.uk

REF	TITLE	PRICE	QTY	TOTAL
1 84101 418 4	Bible Readings for Special Times: Bereavement	£1.99		
1 84101 494 X	Bible Readings for Special Times: Confirmation	£1.99		
1 84101 447 8	Bible Readings for Special Times: Going to College	£1.99		
1 84101 421 4	Bible Readings for Special Times: Ill Health	£1.99		
1 84101 427 3	Bible Readings for Special Times: Marriage	£1.99		
1 84101 457 5	Bible Readings for Special Times: Moving House	£1.99		
1 84101 487 7	Bible Readings for Special Times: New Baby	£1.99		
1 84101 430 3	Bible Readings for Special Times: Retirement	£1.99		

POSTAGE & PACKING CHARGES				
Order value	UK	Europe	Surface	Air Mail
Under £7.00	£1.25	£3.00	£3.50	£5.50
£7.01–£29.99	£2.25	£5.50	£6.50	£10.00
Over £30.00	FREE	Prices on request		

Total Value of books

Postage

TOTAL

Name _____

Account Number (if known) _____

Address _____

_____ Postcode _____

Telephone _____ Email _____

❐ Please email me with information about BRF resources and services

Method of payment:
❐ Cheque ❐ Mastercard ❐ Visa ❐ Postal Order ❐ Maestro

Card no.

☐☐☐☐ ☐☐☐☐ ☐☐☐☐ ☐☐☐☐ ☐☐☐

Issue no. of Switch card ☐☐☐   Expires ☐☐ ☐☐   *Shaded boxes for Maestro use only*

Signature _____

Date ___/___/___

All orders must be accompanied by the appropriate payment.
Please make cheques payable to BRF.

Please send your completed form to:
brf, First Floor, Elsfield Hall,
15–17 Elsfield Way,
Oxford OX2 8FG

PROMO REF: BRST-MH

brf is a Registered Charity